MY LIFE IN THE WILD
OTTER

writer **Meredith Costain**

illustrator **Gary Hanna**

RED LEMON PRESS

I am a sea otter. I have flippers on my hind feet and a thick coat of waterproof fur. My home is the northern and eastern shoreline of the Pacific Ocean, but I rarely come onto land. I use tools to open my food!
Let me tell you my story.

I am born underwater.
Mum brings me up
to the surface.

Then she rolls over and lies on her back in the water, cradling me on her chest to keep me warm. I nestle against her, drinking her sweet, fatty milk.

Mum coos as she fusses over me.
She squeezes the water out of my fur,
then licks it and combs it with her claws.
Then she fluffs it up with her warm breath.

Mum leaves me on my own while she goes off to find food deep down on the ocean floor. She wraps a strand of kelp around me so I won't drift away.

There are many other pups in our raft.
When we're not feeding, we play together.
We roll each other over and over in the
water and practise our grooming skills.

As the sun sets, a shadow falls
across us. It's a sea eagle looking
for dinner. I squeal in terror!

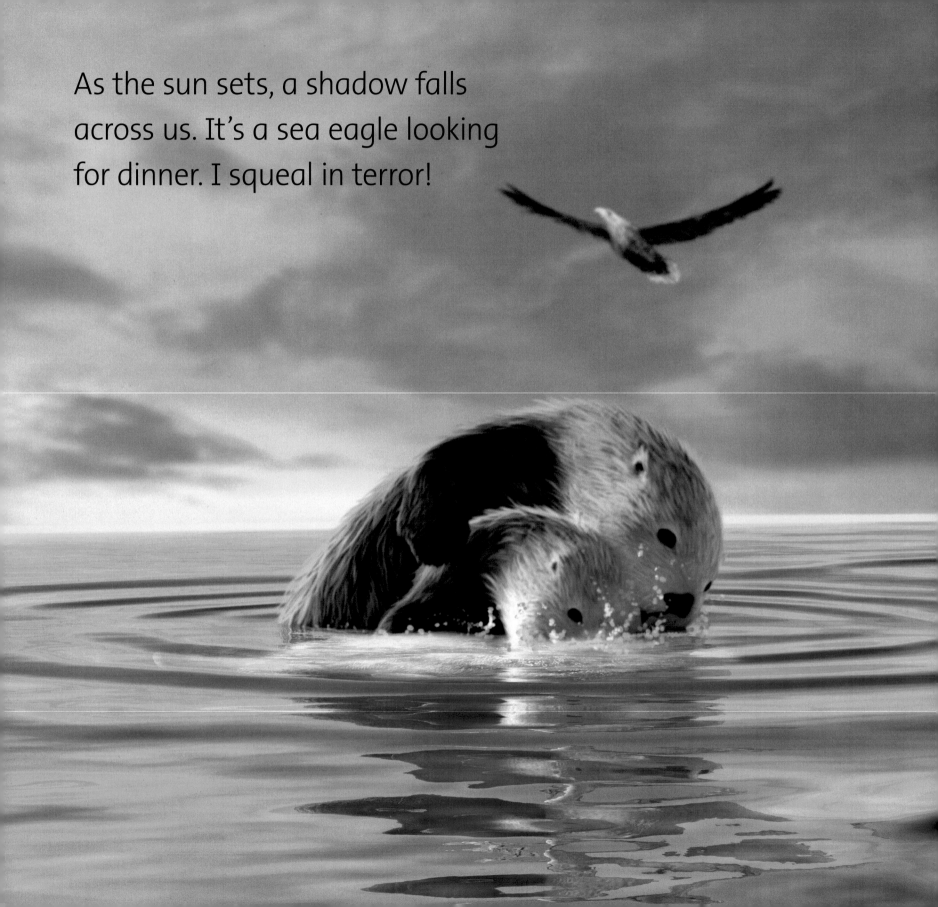

Mum grabs me and together we dive down,
down,
down,
deep under the water, to safety.
When we come back up, the sea eagle has gone.

Mum teaches me how to swim,
dive and gather food.

I see something shiny on the ocean floor and dive down to pick it up. But it's only a pebble. No dinner for me this time.

After our lesson, I'm exhausted.
We settle down to rest. Mum holds my paw
so I don't drift away, out to the open sea.

I'm soon big enough to find food for myself.
I take a deep breath, then dive down to the seabed.

I collect some clamshells and tuck them into the pouch under my forearm. I pick up a rock as well. Then I zoom back up to the surface.

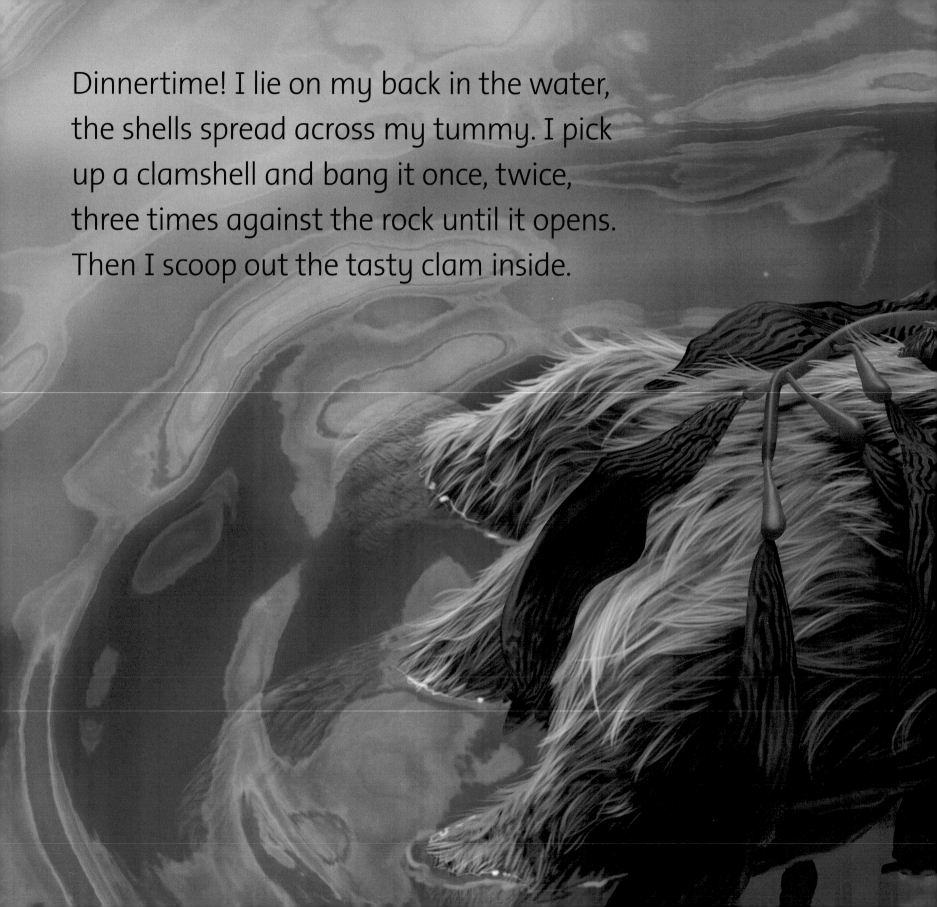

Dinnertime! I lie on my back in the water, the shells spread across my tummy. I pick up a clamshell and bang it once, twice, three times against the rock until it opens. Then I scoop out the tasty clam inside.

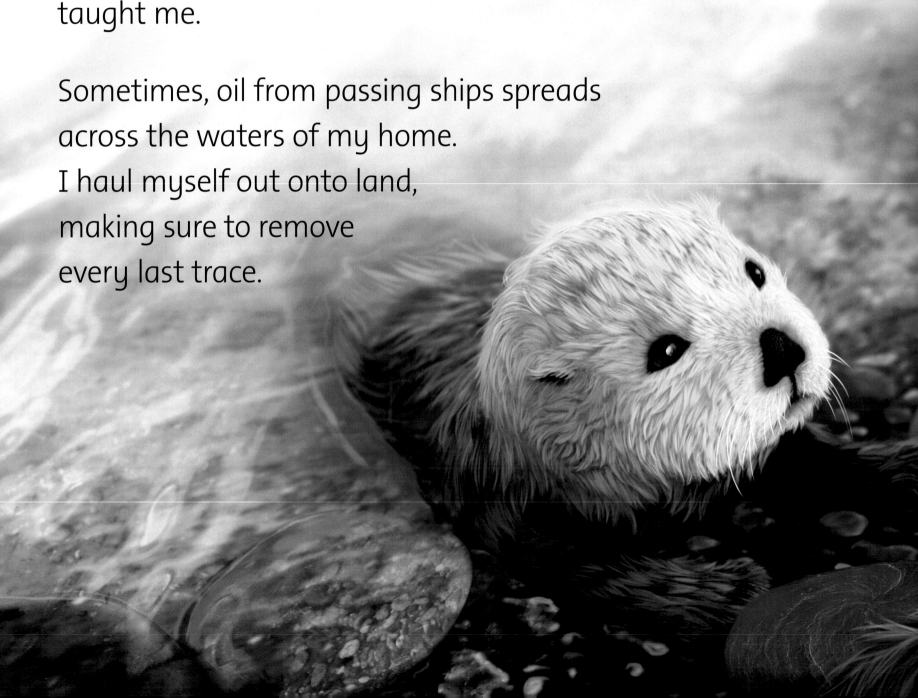

Time passes. I'm now old enough to live on my own. I spend my days grooming my fur and gathering food, using the skills my mother taught me.

Sometimes, oil from passing ships spreads across the waters of my home.
I haul myself out onto land,
making sure to remove
every last trace.

After four summers and winters, I give birth
to my own precious pup. I carry her safely
on my chest as my sisters and I float
together through the kelp, dreaming of
summer days and warm waters full of fish.

Did You Know?

Sea otters are born in the water.

Sea otter pups are born in the water in late winter or early spring. Their eyes are open and they have a full set of milk teeth (baby teeth). A mother has one pup at a time – twins are very rare. She cradles her pup on her chest for the first two months of its life, feeding it milk and keeping it safe and warm.

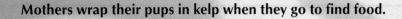

Sea otters have the thickest fur of all mammals.

Sea otter fur has up to a million hairs per square inch (155,000 per cm²). Compare this to a human head, which has only around 100,000 hairs in total! Because they have no blubber, as many other marine animals do, sea otters rely on the air trapped in their thick fur for warmth.

Mothers wrap their pups in kelp when they go to find food.

The kelp stops the young sea otters from drifting away. Sea otters collect food, such as sea urchins, crabs and shellfish, from the ocean floor. They live along the coastline, where the water is rarely deeper than 30 metres (100 ft).

Sea otters live in social groups.

Sea otters live mainly in the water in social groups called rafts. Mothers and pups stay together, with the males in a separate raft, often a long distance away. Playing helps young otters practise skills they will need for survival. Sea otters roll in the water after eating, dislodging food from their fur to ensure it stays waterproof.

Pups squeal to warn their mother that predators are near.

Sea otter predators include sea lions, orcas, sharks and sea eagles. Sea eagles swoop down and snatch sea otter pups from the water's surface. The pups squeal when they are in distress. The high-pitched sound can be heard for miles.

Sea otter pups learn to dive at a young age.

Mothers begin to teach their pups to swim and dive when they are only a few weeks old. Pups need to practise diving for several weeks before they can reach the ocean floor. At first they may bring up only colourful starfish or pebbles, but they soon learn to recognise things they can actually eat.

Did You Know? (continued)

Sea otters hold each other's paws.

In addition to wrapping her pup with strands of kelp, a sea otter mother may hold on to her pup's paw to stop the pup from drifting out to the open ocean while resting or sleeping.

Sea otters store food they have collected on their body.

Sea otters have loose folds of skin under their forearms called 'pouches'. They use these pouches like shopping bags, tucking scallops, sea urchins and crabs into them as they collect them from the ocean floor.

Sea otters use tools to help them eat.

Sea otters lie in the water on their back to eat, using their stomach as a 'table'. They often balance a rock on their chest as well, which they use as a tool to open hard shells. They bang the shell on the rock until it opens enough for them to eat the shellfish inside.

It is essential that sea otters keep their fur clean.

Sea otters spend four to six hours a day grooming their fur and removing food, dirt or oil from it with their paws and claws. If the fur is not kept extremely clean, it will lose the waterproofing qualities that keep sea otters' bodies warm and dry.

Female sea otters are good mothers.

Female sea otters begin to breed when they are around four or five years old. They will have five to six pups in their lifetime. Sometimes, a female will take in an orphaned pup and bring it up as her own.

Meet the Mustelid Family

Sea otters belong to a group of mammals known as mustelids. Here are some other family members:

River otter

Badger

Mink

Ermine

QUIZ

1. Which mustelid looks the most like the sea otter?

2. Which of these mustelids is the largest?

3. Which mustelids have black and white fur?

4. Which mustelid has patterned fur?

Sea otter

Scientific name: *Enhydra lutris*

Coat colour: Dark brown with a creamy grey head, throat and chest

Height: Between 0.9 m and 1.5 meters (3 and 5 feet)

Weight: 20 kg (45 lbs) (female), 29 kg (65 lbs) (male)

Life span: 15 to 20 years (female), 10 to 15 years (male)

Fur: 40,000 to 155,000 per cm² (250,000 to 1,000,000 hairs per in²)

Breath-holding length: Up to 22 minutes

Conservation status: Endangered

Habitat: Coastal waters of the central and north Pacific Ocean

Where sea otters live

Alaska

North Pacific

Sea otter

Pine marten

Weasel

Polecat

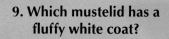

Wolverine

7. Which mustelids have webbed feet?

How many different types of mustelids can you see here?

9. Which mustelid has a fluffy white coat?

8. Which of these mustelids is the smallest?

6. Which mustelid has a short tail?

Glossary

clam   a sea-dwelling animal with a soft body and a hard shell

coo   to make a soft, loving sound

cradle   to hold closely

drift   to be carried away by water

groom   to keep fur clean by licking and pawing

haul   to pull or drag strongly

kelp   coarse brown seaweed

nestle   to lie close or curled next to

pouch   a loose flap of skin under a sea otter's armpit

seabed   the floor of an ocean or sea

RED LEMON PRESS

Published in the UK by:
Red Lemon Press (An imprint of Weldon Owen)
Deepdene Lodge,
Deepdene Avenue,
Dorking,
Surrey RH5 4AT
www.weldonowen.co.uk

Conceived and produced by
Weldon Owen Pty Ltd
Ground Floor 42–44 Victoria Street, McMahons Po[...]
Sydney NSW 2060, Australia
weldonowenpublishing.com

Copyright © 2012 Weldon Owen Pty Ltd

WELDON OWEN PTY LTD
Managing Director Kay Scarlett
Publisher Corinne Roberts
Creative Director Sue Burk
Senior Vice President,
International Sales Stuart Laurence
Sales Manager, North America Ellen Towell
Administration Manager,
International Sales Kristine Ravn

Managing Editor Helen Bateman
Consultant George McKay
Design Concept Cooling Brown Ltd
Designer Gabrielle Green
Images Manager Trucie Henderson
Production Director Todd Rechner
Production and Prepress Controller Mike Crowto[...]
Illustrations Gary Hanna/The Art Agency
except Meet the Mustelid Family pages.

ISBN: 978-1-78342-147-3

Printed and bound in China.

A WELDON OWEN PRODUCTION